P9-DHK-364

a gift *for* ...

from ...

on this date ...

on the occasion *of* ...

LOOK FOR ADDITIONAL PLACES TO
PERSONALIZE THIS BOOK FOR YOUR FRIEND
ON PAGES 11, 21, 35, 47, 59, 69, 83, 95, 113

[WE'LL ALWAYS BE FRIENDS]

the goodbye BOOK

THOMAS NELSON
Since 1798

NASHVILLE   DALLAS   MEXICO CITY   RIO DE JANEIRO   BEIJING

The Goodbye Book
Copyright © 2008 Thomas Nelson, Inc.

All rights reserved. No portion of this publication may be reproduced, stored in a retrieval system, or transmitted by any means—electronic, mechanical, photocopying, recording, or any other—except for brief quotations in printed reviews, without the prior written permission of the publisher.

Published in Nashville, TN, by Thomas Nelson. Thomas Nelson is a trademark of Thomas Nelson, Inc.

Thomas Nelson, Inc., titles may be purchased in bulk for educational, business, fundraising, or sales promotional use. For information, please email SpecialMarkets@ThomasNelson.com.

Unless otherwise indicated, Scripture quotations are taken from The New King James Version. Copyright © 1979, 1980, 1982, Thomas Nelson, Inc.

Scripture quotations marked NIV are taken from the Holy Bible, New International Version®. NIV®. Copyright © 1973, 1978, 1984 by International Bible Society. Used by permission of Zondervan Publishing House. All rights reserved.

Project Editor: Jessica Inman
Designed by Koechel Peterson Design, Minneapolis, Minnesota
ISBN-13: 978-1-4041-0524-9

Printed and bound in China

www.thomasnelson.com

may the road rise up to meet you,
may the wind be ever at your back.
may the sun shine warm upon
your face and the rain fall softly on
your fields. and until we
meet again, may God hold
you in the hollow of His hand.

IRISH BLESSING

don't cry because it's over.
smile because it happened.

THEODORE GEISEL

the best GOODBYE

The book you're holding in your hands means that someone cares about you. It means that you're blessed with someone to miss you. That person is wishing you well as your paths reach a fork and the two of you go in different directions. He or she wants to say goodbye in a tangible way.

And that's the best kind of goodbye, the kind that comes from a dear friend. That kind of goodbye is truly bittersweet, because it fills your mind with memories even as it makes you anticipate a reunion.

May your new path bring you wonderful new friends, and may it find you often in the company of old ones.

how lucky i am to have something that makes saying goodbye so hard.

FROM THE MOVIE *ANNIE* by CAROL SOBIESKI *and* THOMAS MEEHAN

a few favorite

MEMORIES OF OUR TIME TOGETHER:

a true friend unbosoms
freely, advises justly, assists
readily, adventures boldly,
takes all patiently, defends
courageously, and continues
a friend unchangeably.

WILLIAM PENN

YOU WILL ALWAYS BE MY
FAVORITE LUNCH BUDDY.

farewell! God knows when we shall meet again.

WILLIAM SHAKESPEARE

• The final scene of *Casablanca* is a classic goodbye if ever there was one. Rick urges Ilsa, "If that plane leaves the ground and you're not with him, you'll regret it. Maybe not today. Maybe not tomorrow, but soon and for the rest of your life." The plane flies away, taking Ilsa with it, and a few frames later Rick says to Louis, "I think this is the beginning of a beautiful friendship." It just goes to show that just about every ending is in some way a new beginning.

• The Von Trapp kids singing "So Long, Farewell" to their party guests in *The Sound of Music* makes for an elaborate, unforgettable goodbye. Their simple "goodnight" comes replete with choreography and vocal parts carefully assigned to each of the tots. And just try to get that song out of your head.

• The much-parodied final scene between Jack and Rose in 1997's *Titanic* is forever burned on moviegoers' memories. You remember: "I'll never let go, Jack—I'll never let go." Okay, it was a little over the top, but who doesn't love a goodbye that includes a promise never to forget?

friendship is one of the sweetest joys in life. many might have failed beneath the bitterness of their trial had they not found a friend.

CHARLES HADDON SPURGEON

if ever there is tomorrow
when we're not together,
there is something you must
always remember: you are
braver than you believe,
stronger than you seem, and
smarter than you think. but
the most important thing
is, even if we're apart, i'll
always be with you.

A. A. MILNE

gratitude preserves old
friendships, and procures new.

AUTHOR UNKNOWN

i'm so thankful to have a great listener like you as a friend.

what is a
friend?
a single soul
dwelling in
two bodies.

ARISTOTLE

some of my favorite
THINGS WE DO TOGETHER:

• The series finale of *Everybody Loves Raymond* finds Ray in the hospital, his surgeons concerned that he's not waking up from the anesthesia the way he should. After thirty seconds of panic that he might die, his family is relieved to learn that he'll be fine. Back at home, Ray's wife, Debra, is quick with the ice cream and massages, breaking down in tears as she recounts to him her plans for the day, grateful that he's still around. Lesson learned: sometimes we need a little reminder to appreciate the people in our lives.

• In the closing scene of the final episode of *M*A*S*H*—the highest-rated single show of all time—Hawkeye says to B.J., "I know it's tough for you to say goodbye, so I'll say it. Maybe we will see each other again. In any case, I want you to know how much you meant to me." The two men hug, and Hawkeye climbs into a helicopter ready for takeoff. He smiles as he looks down: B.J. has spelled out "Goodbye" with rocks, large enough to be seen from the air.

• The *7th Heaven* series finale (the show's second finale, that is) ended with Eric and Annie deciding to take an RV trip around the country, with their daughter and son-in-law Lucy and Kevin along for the journey. A good formula for a finale involves setting the stage for the characters to move on to new adventures. It's a good way to approach real-life finales as well, with an optimistic eye toward the future.

• When *Friends* ended its ten-year run, the final episode was preceded by an hour of nostalgic interviews and favorite scenes. The real-life application: a good way to end something is by taking a minute (or an hour) to remember, savor, and enjoy.

the future is always
beginning now.

MARK STRAND

THE PEOPLE YOU HAVE YET
TO MEET DON'T KNOW
HOW LUCKY THEY ARE!

christmas is a time when
you get homesick—even
when you're home.

CAROL NELSON

It's the most wonderful time of the year—the time for Christmas cards. There's something about the holiday season that kindles our desire to reconnect with someone we haven't seen in a while. Start your Christmas card list early this year. Make a list of the names and addresses of people you want to keep in touch with despite the changes that might await you in the coming months. Tuck the list somewhere safe until December rolls around, then send a card with a "Hi, how are you?" note. The holiday season just might be the perfect point of contact to help you stay in touch with old friends.

THE BEST THINGS SAID COME
LAST. PEOPLE WILL TALK FOR
HOURS SAYING NOTHING MUCH
AND THEN LINGER AT THE
DOOR WITH WORDS THAT COME
WITH A RUSH FROM THE HEART.

Alan Alda

ever has it been that love
knows not its own depth
until the hour of separation.

KAHLIL GIBRAN

a blessed thing it is for any
man or woman to have a friend,
one human soul whom we can
trust utterly, who knows the best
and worst of us, and who
loves us in spite of all our faults.

CHARLES KINGSLEY

you give
the
very best
presents.

whoever is happy will make others happy too.

ANNE FRANK

the best thing
A FRIEND HAS EVER DONE FOR ME:

to feel rich,
count all the
things you *have*
that money
cannot buy.

ANONYMOUS

that is the best—to laugh with
someone because you both think
the same things are funny.

GLORIA VANDERBILT

one faces the future
with one's past.

PEARL S. BUCK

Starting something new can be a wonderful opportunity to take stock of the past and make decisions for the future. When you think about the last year, what do you think you learned about relationships and life in general? When you think about the year ahead, what do you want to do the same, and what do you want to do differently? Make a list of ways to repeat your successes and achieve new ones in the year ahead.

a friend loves
at all times,
and a brother
is born for
adversity.

PROVERBS 17:17

the greatest
BLESSING

The writer of Ecclesiastes knew the value of friendship.
He wrote, "Two are better than one, . . . for if they fall,
one will lift up his companion" (4:9–10). A friend is a
blessing; a lifelong friend is an even greater one.
Express your gratitude for your friends, and nurture
your friendship so that it lasts a lifetime.

remember, we all stumble,
every one of us. that's why it's a
comfort to go hand in hand.

EMILY KIMBROUGH

your e-mails
are the best.

the most i can do for my friend
is simply be his friend.

HENRY DAVID THOREAU

when we honestly ask ourselves
which person in our lives mean
the most to us, we often find that
it is those who, instead of giving
advice, solutions, or cures,
have chosen rather to share our
pain and touch our wounds with
a warm and tender hand.

HENRI NOUWEN

a good laugh is as good
as a prayer sometimes.

LUCY MAUD MONTGOMERY

the funniest things

THAT HAPPENED WHEN WE WERE TOGETHER:

there is a time for risky love.
there is a time for extravagant
gestures. there is a time to pour
out your affections on one you love.
and when the time comes—
seize it, don't miss it.

MAX LUCADO

the PERFECT MIX

Everyone loves a goodbye mix CD. It's a perfect way to reflect on good memories and say goodbye in a tangible, meaningful way—it's like an audio scrapbook. Here are a few ideas to get you started on a goodbye CD of your own.

- Boyz II Men, "It's So Hard to Say Goodbye to Yesterday"
- Jeff Buckley, "Last Goodbye"
- Simon and Garfunkel, "Homeward Bound"
- Patty Griffin, "Long Ride Home"
- The Beatles, "Hello Goodbye"
- Jim Croce, "Time in a Bottle"
- The Clash, "Should I Stay or Should I Go"
- Enya, "Only Time"
- Peaches and Herb, "Reunited"

be slow in choosing your
friends, slower in changing.

BENJAMIN FRANKLIN

it takes a long time to grow an old friend.

JOHN LEONARD

i like her
because
she smiles
at me and
means it.

ANONYMOUS

i'll never forget the
first day we met.

a friend may well be reckoned
the masterpiece of nature.

RALPH WALDO EMERSON

These lovable, if fictional, friends have so much to teach us about friendship—and they quicken our gratitude for the good friends in our lives.

• Frodo Baggins and Samwise Gamgee. Who could forget Sam's unswerving faithfulness as he accompanies best friend Frodo to take the ring to Mount Doom? In one of the final scenes of Peter Jackson's Lord of the Rings trilogy, Sam picks up his lifelong friend and says, "I can't carry it for you, but I can carry you!"

• Bert and Ernie. A classic pairing somewhat akin to Felix and Oscar or Abbott and Costello. Silly, fun-loving Ernie constantly ruffles the feathers and gets the goat of straitlaced, accountant-like Bert. But the two have their share of sweet moments as well. In the 1978 Christmas special, they pay homage to O. Henry's "The Gift of the Magi" by each selling something they love in order to buy the other a special Christmas present.

• Calvin and Hobbes. Wickedly smart (although perhaps not academically inclined), rather ill-behaved Calvin relies on a buddy like Hobbes to serve alternately as a partner in crime and the voice of reason. The result is a series of unparalleled adventures that make us all wish we had a stuffed tiger to talk to.

a true friend never gets in
your way unless you
happen to be going down.

ARNOLD H. GLASGOW

WE CANNOT HOLD A TORCH TO
LIGHT ANOTHER'S PATH WITHOUT
BRIGHTENING OUR OWN.

Ben Sweetland

encouragement is oxygen to the soul.

GEORGE MATTHEW ADAMS

my favorite
THINGS ABOUT YOU:

sir, more than kisses, letters mingle souls; for, thus friends absent speak.

JOHN DONNE

the lines
OF COMMUNICATION

Fret not. It's easier than ever to keep in touch with friends across the miles. E-mail, blogging, photo sharing and social networking Web sites—you have plenty of tools right at your computer keyboard. Of course, there's no substitute for an old-fashioned card or letter, something physical and personal that lets a friend know you've taken time out of your day to say hello. So as you journey forward, stock up on stationery. Staying connected to friends old and new will make the journey even richer and better.

shared joy is a double joy;
shared sorrow is half a sorrow.

SWEDISH PROVERB

i felt it shelter
to speak
to you.

EMILY DICKINSON

LET US BE GRATEFUL TO PEOPLE
WHO MAKE US HAPPY, THEY ARE
THE CHARMING GARDENERS
WHO MAKE OUR SOULS BLOSSOM.

Marcel Proust

having you as a friend has made my days more interesting, more full of life, and much more fun.

greater love has no one
than this, than to lay down
one's life for his friends.

JOHN 15:13

The best friendships are through-thick-and-thin, come-what-may friendships. In the Bible, David and Jonathan had just that kind of friendship. Jonathan even thwarted his own father's plans to kill David, and 1 Samuel 20:17 says that Jonathan loved David "as he loved his own soul." Their friendship was the kind with staying power; and staying power just requires a little determination.

nothing but heaven itself is better than a friend who is really a friend.

PLAUTUS

i'll always
REMEMBER YOU AS:

keep some souvenirs of your past, or how will you ever prove it wasn't all a dream?

ASHLEIGH BRILLIANT

a picture
IS WORTH A THOUSAND WORDS

There's no better way to remember good times with good friends than through pictures. You don't have to be a master of scrapbooks to gather some favorite photos—posed, candid, and everything in between—to help you keep happy memories alive. Frame them. Fasten them to your refrigerator with magnets. Make them into a collage. Put them anywhere you'll see them often and be reminded of the blessing of friends.

security in a relationship lies neither in looking back to what it was in nostalgia, nor forward to what it might be in dread or anticipation, but living in the present relationship and accepting it as it is now.

ANNE MORROW LINDBERGH

THE BEST MIRROR
IS AN OLD FRIEND.

English Proverb

Not all of these buddy movies can be taken too seriously, but

they're all great for reminding us that friendship makes life

fun, funny, and above all, absolutely wonderful.

• *A Charlie Brown Christmas.* So much friendship and
nostalgia packed into thirty short minutes. Charlie Brown
discovers the true meaning of Christmas with a little help
from Linus, Snoopy, and the rest of the Peanuts gang—even
Lucy gets in on the act—all set to one of the most memorable
and winsome soundtracks in Christmas-special history.

• *The Sisterhood of the Traveling Pants.* One seemingly magical pair of jeans, one special summer, and four best friends: the ultimate recipe for adventure. As Lena, Carmen, Bridget, and Tibby learn life lessons and come of age, they remind us that nothing good happens in our lives without good friends.

• *The Lord of the Rings* trilogy. A fellowship of nine set out on a do-or-die mission, which proves to be a test of their loyalty, will, and courage and a testament to the value of self-sacrifice. But perhaps the brightest spot in these films are the charming antics of mischievous buddies Merry and Pippin.

• *Shrek.* On the surface, it appears that Donkey serves solely to try Shrek's patience with incessant questions and pleas for affirmation. But without the affable equine, Shrek would have missed out on an adventure or three, several self-realizations, and probably his princess.

a loyal friend laughs at your jokes
when they're not so good, and
sympathizes with your problems
when they're not so bad.

ARNOLD H. GLASGOW

thank you for always making
me feel like a priority.

friendship is unnecessary, like philosophy, like art, like the universe itself (for God did not need to create). it has no survival value; rather it is one of those things that give value to survival.

C. S. LEWIS

the best GIFTS

Sometimes it's hard to find the words to say goodbye.

Maybe that's why goodbye gifts come in so handy—they're

nonverbal ways to say, "I've loved being friends with you,

and I'll miss you." But don't forget about "I remember you"

gifts. A card or small gift for a friend you haven't seen in a

while is a wonderful way to say, "I'm still thinking of you."

What better way to keep a meaningful friendship alive?

cherish your human connections: your relationships with friends and family.

BARBARA BUSH

Near the end of *It's a Wonderful Life*, after being snatched

from despair by the generosity of friends and an angel named

Clarence, Jimmy Stewart's George Bailey reads one last

message from his guardian angel: "Remember, no man is a

failure who has friends." That's a message we could all take

to heart. No matter where our paths might take us,

nothing will ever be more important than the people with

whom we share the journey.

if we all did the things
we are capable of doing,
we would literally
astound ourselves.

THOMAS ALVA EDISON

i know you're headed
for great things.

the friendship is not a reward
for our discrimination and
good taste in finding one another
out. it is the instrument by
which God reveals to each the
beauties of all the others.

C. S. LEWIS

what i'll miss

MOST ABOUT YOU:

every time you smile at someone,
it is an action of love, a gift to that
person, a beautiful thing.

MOTHER TERESA

life minus
love equals
nothing.

GEORGE SWEETING

in the end, it's not the years
in your life that count.
it's the life in your years.

ABRAHAM LINCOLN

the value
OF A GOOD FRIEND

We all know friends make life fuller, but research suggests that having good friends around might actually extend our lives. An Australian study among the elderly found that those who reported regular contact with friends had a greater survival rate than those without a strong social network. All the more reason to cherish the friends who have blessed our lives.

a good friend is
cheaper than therapy.

AUTHOR UNKNOWN

thanks for always helping me see things a little more clearly.

I MUST FEEL PRIDE IN MY FRIEND'S
ACCOMPLISHMENTS AS IF THEY WERE MINE.

Ralph Waldo Emerson

a word
OF ENCOURAGEMENT

The greatest role any friend or family member can play in our lives is that of encourager. We all need someone to cheer us up and help us along when life gets difficult, and even when things are running smoothly. Reach out to those around you with a little encouragement—a note, a word of thanks, a word of affirmation, maybe even a batch of cookies. Encouragement will comfort and strengthen friends old and new.

a friend is someone who
understands your past, believes
in your future, and accepts you
today just the way you are.
a friend is someone with whom
you dare to be yourself.

C. RAYMOND BERAN

there is always
an intangible
something which
makes a friend, it
is not what he does,
but what he is.

OSWALD CHAMBERS

every action in our lives
touches on some chord that
will vibrate in eternity.

EDWIN HUBBEL CHAPIN

i'll always

BE GRATEFUL TO YOU FOR:

Sometimes it's hard to say goodbye. But there are ways to let friends know how much they've meant to us over the years:

• Throw a Party. Getting everyone together one last time can be a wonderful—if bittersweet—way to close a chapter. Go out to dinner, watch some favorite DVDs, or just sit and talk. Reminisce a little and be sure to exchange new contact information, and you'll make your friendship even stronger.

• Write a Letter. It's personal, it's heartfelt, and it can be kept in a drawer forever. A good goodbye letter recounts favorite memories, encourages the recipient with hope about the future, and again, includes new contact information. Just a little time spent with paper and a pen will give your friend something to remember forever.

• Make a Scrapbook. Photos are perfect goodbye gifts, and a scrapbook of favorite memories lets a good friend know just what you've loved about hanging out together. It doesn't have to be professional—just photos and captions and a few comforting words will do.

• Make a Care Package. Nothing beats a surprise care package. Snacks, hot drink mixes, office supplies, and whatever else your friends might need in the coming days and weeks, all bundled together with a note from you, will absolutely make their day, no matter how far away they are.

we do not understand the
intricate pattern of the stars
in their courses, but we know
that He who created them does,
and that just as surely as He
guides them, He is charting
a safe course for us.

BILLY GRAHAM

THE UNCERTAINTIES OF
THE PRESENT ALWAYS GIVE WAY
TO THE ENCHANTED
POSSIBILITIES OF THE FUTURE.

Gelsey Kirkland

i can no other answer make,
but, thanks, and thanks.

WILLIAM SHAKESPEARE

i will definitely never forget you.

God gave us memories that we might have roses in December.

J. M. BARRIE

time CAPSULE

The only way to hold on to good times is to remember them. And there are plenty of ways to do that. In addition to framing and scrapbooking pictures, you can make CDs of all the songs you listened to while spending time with a special someone. Scent is also incredibly powerful. Save a little of the scent you were wearing during a fun time in your life, and every time you smell it, you'll remember those good times.

As you reminisce, take a minute to be thankful for the fun you've had in the past—and the good times that lie ahead in the future.

hold a true friend
with both hands.

NIGERIAN PROVERB

In the "Rockumentary" episode of *Saved by the Bell* (if you were born after 1970, don't even pretend you've never seen this show), Zack dreams that he and the Bayside gang have formed a band called Zack Attack, and Casey Kasem guest stars to narrate their "rockumentary." There are creative differences and a dramatic breakup, of course—but by the end of the show, everyone is back onstage, singing their theme song, "Friends Forever." The moral of the story? No matter what happens, it's never too late to reunite with old friends.

life becomes harder for us when
we live for others, but it also
becomes richer and happier.

ALBERT SCHWEITZER

be kindly affectionate to one another with brotherly love, in honor
giving preference to one another.

ROMANS 12:10

to send a letter is a good way to go somewhere without moving anything but your heart.

PHYLLIS THEROUX

don't forget TO WRITE

No matter where you're going in the coming weeks and

months, postcards are available pretty much everywhere.

A glossy photo depicting some element of your new

surroundings—the Eiffel Tower, an Ivy League school, or

the world's tallest termite mound—combined with a short

"thinking of you" message will make a friend's day. Sure, it's

touristy, but that's half the fun.

what you get by achieving your goals is not as important as what you become by achieving your goals.

ZIG ZIGLAR

i'm so proud
of the person
i've seen you
become.

as iron sharpens iron,
so one man sharpens another.

PROVERBS 27:17 NIV

you've helped me grow in so many ways, LIKE . . .

all changes, even the most longed for, have their melancholy; for what we leave behind us is a part of ourselves; we must die to one life before we can enter another.

ANATOLE FRANCE

CHANGE ALWAYS COMES BEARING GIFTS.

Price Pritchett

hitch your
wagon
to a star.

RALPH WALDO EMERSON

Don't worry about the future. Sure, it's hard to say goodbye to friends, and change can be difficult. But there are bright days ahead. You won't lose your friends forever, and you have new friendships and new adventures ahead of you.

If you're feeling a little change-weary, make a gratitude list: write down all the good things in your life right now, the good things you've experienced in the past, and the good things you anticipate for the future. And in the days ahead, don't be surprised if you encounter a few blessings you never saw coming.

the language of friendship is
not words but meanings.

HENRY DAVID THOREAU

We don't know who first came up with the idea of signing one another's class yearbooks. It's just something we do. Just about every yearbook includes one or more of the old standbys—

- The very obvious "Have a good summer."
- The ubiquitous "What a long, strange trip it's been."
- The formula "Stay" plus a favorable adjective, followed by an exclamation point: "Stay smart!" "Stay sweet!" "Stay cute!" This one might be more meaningful if it weren't so short.
- A brand-new round of yearbook poems seem to crop up every year, some sweet, some . . . not so sweet.

The best yearbook inscriptions are those little paragraphs that tell you what the autograph writer liked about you, the ones that say, "I'll miss you" and "I wish you the best." Those are the ones we read fondly long after graduation, the ones that make our day even years later.

like branches on a tree,
we grow in different directions,
yet our roots remain as one.
each of our lives will always be a
special part of the other.

AUTHOR UNKNOWN

no one will ever take your place at
parties. who else knows
all the words to every Christmas
song ever written?

be the living expression of God's kindness: kindness in your face, kindness in your eyes, kindness in your smile, kindness in your warm greeting.

MOTHER TERESA

be kind. remember that everyone you meet is fighting a hard battle.

HARRY THOMPSON

love has been called the most
effective motivational force in all
the world. when love is at work
in us, it is remarkable how giving
and forgiving, understanding
and tolerant we can be.

CHARLES SWINDOLL

the kindness
OF SPIDERS

In E. B. White's *Charlotte's Web* (and the subsequent
movies), Charlotte the spider befriends Wilbur the pig.
Even though they form an unlikely pair, Charlotte shows
great kindness to Wilbur, saving his life nearly at the expense
of her own. In this tale, the arachnid with a heart of gold ends
up giving us one of the most iconic examples of friendship
in all of literature.

having someone who understands
is a great blessing for ourselves.
being someone who understands is
a great blessing to others.

JANETTE OKE

I'LL ALWAYS BE GRATEFUL
FOR THE BLESSING
OF KNOWING YOU.

the Lord bless you and keep you;
the Lord make His face
shine upon you,
and be gracious to you;
the Lord lift up His
countenance upon you,
and give you peace.

NUMBERS 6:24–26